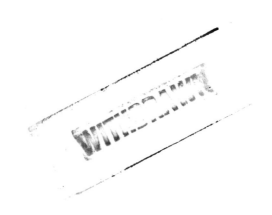

THE MOST INFLUENTIAL FEMALE WRITERS

BREAKING THE GLASS CEILING
THE MOST INFLUENTIAL WOMEN™

THE MOST INFLUENTIAL
FEMALE
WRITERS

ANNE CUNNINGHAM

Rosen
YA
New York

Published in 2019 by The Rosen Publishing Group, Inc.
29 East 21st Street, New York, NY 10010

Cataloging-in-Publication Data

Names: Cunningham, Anne, author.
Title: The most influential female writers / Anne Cunningham.
Description: New York : Rosen Publishing, 2019. | Series: Breaking the glass ceiling: The most influential women | Includes bibliographical references and index. | Audience: Grades 7–12.
Identifiers: ISBN 9781508179665 (library bound) | ISBN 9781508179818 (pbk.)
Subjects: LCSH: Women authors—Biography—Juvenile literature.
Classification: LCC PN471.C86 2018 | DDC 809'.89287—dc23

Manufactured in the United States of America

On the cover: Maya Angelou is pictured here in 2010. Angelou's words soar, shedding light on oppression and inspiring women to speak out about their endeavors to conquer bias, discrimination, and exploitation.

CONTENTS

INTRODUCTION

When the high priestess Enheduanna composed her "Sumerian Temple Hymns" in the ancient Mesopotamian city of Ur around 2300 BCE, she had no idea that her activities would earn her the distinction of being the world's first female author and the first author known by name in world history. It is similarly unlikely that Murasaki Shikibu suspected her book *The Tale of Genji* (1021), a realistic rendering of aristocratic court life in eleventh-century Japan, would later be considered the world's first novel.

These authors illustrate the trailblazing role women have played in literature since the invention of writing. Across every genre and historical period, women have produced a dizzying array of writing addressing all aspects of human experience. But women's writing has often been considered merely a collection of curiosities and footnotes of interest only to historians. The literary critic Linda Woodbridge summarizes this misconception, stating that men "inhabit literature land; women inhabit history-land." The tendency to categorize writing by women as *women's writing* ignores the diversity of women's experience and the socially constructed nature of gender. While acknowledging the historical and material disadvantages women writers have grappled with, this survey of the world's

Novelist, critic, and essayist Virginia Woolf was a member of the Bloomsbury group, a literary salon based in London. Her extended essay *A Room of One's Own* is a key work of feminism, and her novels, such as *To the Lighthouse* and *Mrs. Dalloway*, are essential modernist texts.

most influential female authors places women in the center of the discussion about the evolution of literature and writing.

The thread that unites women writers throughout the ages is the common need to write within institutionalized systems of male dominance we know as patriarchies. Returning to the example of Enheduanna, her hymns were foremost pragmatic texts designed to influence her political situation. By merging the competing deities of the Akkadians with the Sumerians, her writing helped stabilize her father's empire. An educated daughter of the ruling class, Enheduanna served the needs of the dominant and increasingly patriarchal social order to which she belonged. At the same time, her skillful use of figurative language in praise of the goddess Inanna demonstrated both her aesthetic prowess and spiritual commitments. The tension between a female author's social role and her individuality begins with the first author ever, and has not yet gone away.

Gender is just one factor informing the writing of authors, and traits such as race, class, religion, sexuality, and nationality come into play as well. These differences complicate any easy equivalence between all women. In Reformation England, for example, differing interpretations of scripture divided women far more than any common notion of womanhood united them. In *A Room of One's Own,* Virginia Woolf imagines that William Shakespeare had a sister named Judith. Struggling to write in a male-dominated society, Judith commits suicide. While Woolf's tale is an illuminating parable of sexism and writing, it ignores the fact that educated women during the English Renaissance would have seen William Shakespeare's profession as beneath them.

The professionalization of writing is an early-modern phenomenon. Aphra Behn, writing in the seventeenth century, is the first female practitioner of this new trade. In the Middle Ages, daughters of noble families displaying a proclivity toward reading and writing were, if possible, sent to convents to further their education. While such a fate may appear cruel to us, the convent spared gifted women like Hildegard of Bingen and Hrotsvit von Gandersheim from the demands of family life and childrearing and allowed them to pursue their intellectual interests. From this angle, the religious cloisters of the Middle Ages can be viewed as progressive institutions.

The literary marketplace has grown tremendously since early-modern times, and the availability of works by women from around the world has never been greater. Since the dawn of recorded history, women writers have created some of the world's best literature, significantly shaping intellectual, cultural, and political landscapes. Yet the history of female writers is often neglected and undervalued. This book illuminates not only the vital work of so many brilliant female writers, but also sheds light on the differences and commonalities these authors faced as women. All of the women you will encounter in this book made unique and lasting contributions to writing. They are acknowledged and appreciated for their influential mark on literature and culture above all else.

CHAPTER ONE

WOMEN OF THE ANCIENT WORLD

The ancient world describes the period from the seventh century BCE to roughly the sixth century CE. The story of human writing begins then. Cuneiform script was first developed in ancient Mesopotamia, though there is evidence that other cultures such as Egyptian and Chinese invented writing independently. Within a few centuries, writers from Greece and Rome were producing dramas, epic poems, and other works on topics such as astronomy, history, medicine, philosophy, and travel.

The Greco-Roman world declined with the rise of Christianity, and ended with the fall of the Roman Empire in the fifth century CE. Geographically, the ancient world extended from Spain to the Middle East and as far south as Egypt. Highly literate

This is an example of a cuneiform tablet (ca. 1632 BCE). Ancient Babylonians used a wedge-shaped stylus to inscribe these clay tablets, which contain some of the world's oldest writing.

civilizations also existed in what is now known as East Asia. Very few women could read and write in ancient China and Japan. Still, some of the earliest known novels and poems written by women come to us from that part of the world.

The Greek biographer and essayist Plutarch wrote that a woman "should be modest and careful about saying anything in the hearing of people who aren't family, since this would be exposing herself." The antiquated notion that women's lives and thoughts should remain private originates in the ancient world. Many women in ancient societies were denied access to literacy. And the women who could read and write tended to be from the aristocracy. Therefore, women produced less writing than men in ancient times. Furthermore, much writing by women has not survived, and scholars have trouble determining whether a work was written by a man or by a woman.

Despite the imbalance in literary output between women and men in the ancient world, women did write on a broad range of subjects. Their writing sometimes changed the world in which they lived. Enheduanna and Lady Xu Mu both used writing to influence political events, while Sappho's lyric poetry was well regarded in its day. Although the ancient world was dominated by men, women used their thoughts and words to engage with the world and affect change. They produced literature of enduring interest and value.

Enheduanna, the World's First Author

Located between the Tigris and Euphrates rivers in what is now modern-day Iraq, ancient Mesopotamia is known as the "cradle of civilization" because the earliest known city-states emerged there. The Sumerians were the first people to settle this area about seven thousand years ago. Using a reed stylus, Sumerian scribes etched wedge-shaped marks into clay tablets. This technique, known as cuneiform, emerged around 3100 BCE, and is the earliest known form of writing.

The Sumerians lived in the south of ancient Mesopotamia, sharing the land with another group in the north called the Akkadians. Under the rule of Sargon the Great (2334–2279 BCE), the Akkadians conquered and unified Mesopotamia, creating the first empire in the ancient world. Sargon the Great rose to power around 2300 BCE and established the city of Akkad. Sumerian rivals from the city of Uruk attacked Akkad, but Sargon's forces repelled the attack. In response, Sargon conquered Uruk and Ur, then the capital of civilization.

Each city-state in ancient Mesopotamia had particular gods and a temple where priests and priestesses mediated between the gods and humans. The Ziggurat of Ur, located in the city of Ur, was a shrine for the important Sumerian deities Nanna, the moon god, and Inanna, goddess of fertility, love, political power, and war. The Akkadians worshipped different deities than the Sumerians. Such inconsistency among deities was an obstacle to Sargon as he attempted to unify and stabilize an empire.

The burden of bridging these spiritual and political divides fell on Sargon's daughter, Enheduanna. Under her father's rule, Enheduanna was elevated to the role of high priestess of Ur and became the first author known to the world by name. Her writing successfully merged Sumerian gods with their Akkadian counterparts and thus altered beliefs about the divine. A creative, highly educated, and politically engaged woman, Enheduanna represented a strong female presence capable of fulfilling a diverse set of social roles in the ancient world.

Enheduanna's literary corpus consists of a few major works. "The Sumerian Temple Hymns" is a collection of forty-two hymns addressed to various temples throughout ancient Sumer, and remained in use for centuries after her death. Around 2350 BCE, Enheduanna faced a challenge from Sumerian rebels who exiled her from Ur. *The Exaltation of Inanna* was a passionate appeal to the goddess Inanna to reinstate Enheduanna as priestess and to defeat her foes. In the poem "The Banishment from Ur," Enheduanna writes, "I the high priestess Enheduanna! / I carried the ritual basket and sang / Your praise / Now I am banished among the lepers." As these lines demonstrate, Enheduanna often identified herself in the first person throughout her poetry, a signifier of pride. Her temporarily diminished status wounded this pride and led to her appeal for cosmic justice.

Sappho

The Greco-Roman period of classical antiquity begins with the rise of Greek city-states around the seventh century BCE and continues until the fall of the Roman Empire in the fifth century CE. The genre most closely associated with this period is epic poetry, which was typically written by men. Although there are only about one hundred known women writers from this period, a surprising range and diversity of women's writing from the classical period exists, including history, lyric poetry, mathematics, and philosophy.

Sappho was born on the Greek island of Lesbos around 630 BCE to an upper-class family. Few details about Sappho's life are known for certain. Much of what we know about Sappho's life comes from her work. Sappho's work enables scholars to sketch an outline of her life, but little else. She had three brothers, and she ran an academy for unmarried young women in Mytilene, the largest city on the island of Lesbos. She is said to have married a wealthy man named Circylas, with whom she had a daughter named Kleis (possibly named after her mother), but scholars disagree about this. Complicating the picture of Sappho's life is that much of her work has not survived. Still, Sappho is the most famous female writer of antiquity.

This bust of the Greek poet Sappho is made of black basalt and dates from the sixth century BCE. The sculpture depicts Sappho's attractive, somewhat intense gaze.

Only about 650 of the estimated 10,000 lines Sappho wrote survive. Her "Ode to Aphrodite" is the only complete poem we have from her. Sappho's poetry was meant to be sung with accompaniment from a lyre, hence her work is lyric poetry. Her poetry includes decorous, descriptive language rife with sensual allusions. Images of beauty and luxury permeate her lines alongside allusions to the gods and heroes of Greek mythology. Her poems are mostly about love and desire.

A hallmark of Sappho's poetry is her frank discussion of love between women. And the term "lesbian" comes from name of the island Sappho called home. Recently, critics have cautioned against reading too much homoeroticism into Sappho's work, however, as this can obscure the context of her poems. One of her most homoerotic poems is actually a wedding song. According to the conventions of ancient Greek weddings, the bride was supposed to be desirable to all men and women present. Such historical grounding complicates a reading in which the author's sexuality determines the content of her work.

Julia Balbilla

Julia Balbilla was a member of the Roman aristocracy known for her poetry. In 130 CE, Balbilla accompanied the emperor of Rome Hadrian and his wife Sabina on a trip to see the statue of Memnon in Thebes, Egypt. Balbilla inscribed four poems onto the statue. This led to dismissals of her work as graffiti. However, she inscribed her verse with the full approval of the emperor, and intended her writing to be legible and meaningful to the general public.

Ironically, Balbilla's poetry shares a tendency toward self-aggrandizement common among contemporary graffiti artists. She made boasting reference to her noble heritage and to the lasting

WOMEN'S LETTERS IN ANCIENT EGYPT

Women enjoyed a relatively high status in ancient Egypt, and legendary queens such as Hatshepsut, Nefertiti, and Cleopatra are major figures in world history. Even common Egyptian women shared the same basic rights as men. Egyptian women could own property, and unlike Greek and Roman women, they could travel without male accompaniment.

One area of inequality between Egyptian men and women was education. Literacy, even among men, was not widespread in ancient Egypt, so very few women wrote or were employed as scribes. The Egyptian women tended to write personal letters. Hundreds of letters by ancient Egyptian women survive today on pottery and papyrus. In these letters, women describe their habits and everyday experiences, and even discuss legal, economic, and political issues.

power of her poetry. In an attempt to honor her friends Hadrian and Sabina, Balbilla used verse to describe a kinship between the hero Memnon and the visiting Romans. She writes, "When he saw Hadrian, the king of all / Before the rays of the sun / He greeted him— as far as he was able." This line was perhaps an allusion to the statue, which had fallen into disrepair.

Aelia Eudocia

Aelia Eudocia was a Greek-born poet who became Empress of the Byzantine Empire upon her marriage to Emperor Theodosius II in 421 CE. Her epic poetry dealt with Christian themes. Only a small percentage of her work survives. The lack of a complete collection of her writing has frustrated scholars and caused Eudocia's work to be understudied.

Eudocia was born around 400 CE in Athens, Greece, with the given name Athenais. Her father Leontius, a philosopher and teacher of Rhetoric at the Academy of Athens, gave his daughter instructed her in Greek, Latin, poetry, and oration. When her father died, he left most of the inheritance to Eudocia's brothers. At the urging of an aunt with whom she was living, Eudocia traveled to Constantinople, then the capitol of the Eastern Roman Empire, to ask the emperor to correct this injustice. Though she only had one hundred coins when she arrived in Constantinople, she soon attracted the attention of Emperor Theodosius. The two were married in 421

Empress Aelia Eudocia was born in Athens (ca. 401) and married Emperor Theodosius II of Byzantium. Here she is depicted with her court.

CE, at which point Eudocia took the name Aelia.

The ruling couple of Constantinople enjoyed a few smooth years. Eudocia continued to write, helped found a university, and had two children. However, tensions flared between Eudocia and her sister-in-law, Pulcheria. Eudocia advocated for religious freedom for Jews, which Pulcheria, a fanatic Christian, opposed. After returning to Constantinople from a pilgrimage to Jerusalem, Eudocia was falsely accused of adultery, and her alleged lovers were banished and executed. She retaliated by hiring an assassin to kill the executioner. Eudocia dedicated the remainder of her life to writing poetry. Unfortunately, only a few of her complete poems remain.

Lady Xu Mu of Ancient China

Lady Xu Mu of the Ji clan is the first poet recorded in ancient Chinese history. Hailing from Dingjing, capital of the Chinese state Wei, Lady Xu Mu was born in 690 BCE, making her Sappho's contemporary. Unlike Sappho's, much of Lady Xu Mu's work engaged with the politics of her time and place. Her most famous poem, "Speeding Chariot," criticizes state policies that left her province in danger. Around the time of Lady Xu Mu's birth, the state of Wei was at war. Lady Xu Mu wanted to marry the emperor of the powerful neighboring state of Qi to solidify diplomatic ties. Her parents objected, however, and she instead married Duke Mu, of Xu. Her marriage required her to move far from home, which inspired her melancholy poems "Bamboo Pole" and "Spring Water." Lady Xu Mu was a patriot, and her poems were read widely, both in her day and by successive generations.

CHAPTER TWO

LIGHTING UP THE DARK AGES

The Middle Ages in European history lasted for about a thousand years. They began with the fall of the Roman Empire in the fifth century and ended with the Renaissance in the fourteenth century. The Middle Ages is divided into the Early, High, and Late Middle Ages. A common conception of the Middle Ages is that they were dogged by war, famine, and plague, and that the Catholic Church hindered the development of the arts and sciences in Europe. The Middle Ages are often called the "Dark Ages." While there is some truth in this characterization, it does not give a full picture of this dynamic age.

The High Middle Ages represent a high-water mark for women writers. The High Middle Ages lasted from the eleventh to the thirteenth century. Population increased rapidly during this time, alongside improvements in agriculture and medicine. These technical advances fostered the social and political stability that nurture philosophical and literary pursuits. Women such as Hrotsvit von Gandersheim, Hildegard of Bingen, and Héloïse wrote during the High Middle Ages. Though there were a handful of notable female writers in the Late Middle Ages, plague and political schisms created conditions unfavorable to literacy. The fascinating lives and innovative works women produced during the High Middle Ages counter the notion that the Middle Ages were merely a dark age.

Hrotsvit von Gandersheim

Hrotsvit von Gandersheim was a tenth-century German writer of prose, poems, and plays. Her six Christian plays make her the world's first female playwright. Hrotsvit also wrote eight legends and two epics, making her the most accomplished European female poet since Sappho. Hrotsvit's works are collected in three books marked by three distinct creative phases.

Hrotsvit was born around 930 and was of noble Saxon descent. She was a canoness at a convent in Gandersheim, which was the center of culture and education in the Ottonian dynasty. Canonesses took vows of obedience and chastity like a nun, but they were not required to take a vow of poverty. Hrotsvit studied during a golden age. She received a classical education and read Virgil, Horace, and Ovid. Details

Hrotsvit von Gandersheim was a German canoness and poet. In this historical illustration, she reads her legends to fellow residents of a convent in what is now Bad Gandersheim, Germany.

of Hrotsvit's life are sketchy. Most biographical information comes from the prefaces to her books and letters. Hrotsvit may have had some worldly experiences before she embraced Benedictine spirituality, but as a canoness she valued solitude in worship and martyrdom. These Christian ideals are recurrent themes in her writing.

Hrotsvit's first book collects legends written in Leonine verse, a Latin poetic form that uses internal rhymes and was devised by the Latin monk Leoninus. The first legend is called *Maria* and is an orthodox treatment of the life of the Virgin Mary. Book one also includes Hrotsvit's famous legend *Theophilius*, the story of a man who consults a Jewish sorcerer and the devil for assistance with his career. The legend illustrates the devil's powerful influence in the world and the struggle between good and evil. These traditional religious themes informed much of Hrotsvit's subsequent work.

Hrotsvit's second and most famous volume contains six hagiographic plays written in rhyming, rhythmic prose. Hagiographic literature is based on the lives of saints and other religious figures. The plays are meant to impart moral lessons. For example, the play *Dulcitius* presents story of three virgin sisters, Agape, Chionia, and Hirena, who are each pledged to chastity. Dulcitius tries to seduce the sisters, who unite in prayer against their pursuer. Dulcitius mistakes cooking implements for the women. When he embraces the pots and pans, his face is smeared with ash, and he is chased from the premises. This plot twist uses medieval "kitchen humor" to convey the moral lesson Hrotsvit wished to impart.

Hrotsvit's third volume contains two epics written in Latin hexameter, *Gesta Oddonis Imperatori* and *Primordia*. The epics provide histories of the Ottonian dynasty and Hrotsvit's individual order.

Hrotsvit is remembered as the earliest German woman writer. Although she believed that men were inherently better writers than women, her remarkable body of work challenges that idea.

Hildegard of Bingen

Hildegard of Bingen was a Benedictine abbess, mystic visionary, and leading Christian theologian of the eleventh century. She began having mystical religious visions at the age of five. At age forty-two, she claimed God ordered her to "write down that which you see and hear." Although she seldom spoke of her visions before this divine injunction, she discussed them with Jutta, her instructor and mentor, and also with a respected monk named Volmar. Seeking additional advice, Hildegard wrote to the French abbot Bernard of Clairvaux, who encouraged her to write and cautioned her against interfering with God's will by repressing her insights. Finally, Hildegard received official approval from Pope Eugene III. Although she was shy and humble, such support emboldened Hildegard to describe her powerful visions in writing.

Thus, she embarked on the most extraordinary writing career of any woman during the Middle Ages. Hildegard was also a polymath who excelled in many subjects and genres. She wrote extensively about the human body and herbal medicine and was also a playwright and songwriter. Her vocal-based compositions are still in print and are respected by musicologists. Hildegard's works have intrigued scholars for nearly a millennium. Her books appeal to religious scholars, historians, and readers interested in new-age spirituality.

Hildegard was born in Bermersheim, Germany, in 1098. Her father Hildebert von Bermersheim was a knight, and her mother Mechthilde was of the nobility. Hildegard was the last of ten children. She was educated in the Benedictine tradition at a monastery in St. Disibode. At age eighteen, she took the vows to become a nun. Within twenty years she was in charge of the entire female half of the monastery. According to the monk Godfrey, who was Hildegard's first biographer, this period of Hildegard's life was successful but uneventful. Godfrey describes Hildegard as a soft-spoken and exceedingly virtuous young woman.

In 1142, Hildegard began composing the first of the three books based on her visions that became her magnum opus. The first book, *Scivias*, which suggests to "Know the Ways of the Lord," was completed in 1151. In the text, Hildegard recounts her mystical interpretation of Christian theological elements such as the creation of the universe, Adam

German abbess Hildegard von Bingen was a remarkable polymath. Her *Book of Divine Works* interprets her mystical visions in biblical terms. She was also a skilled musician, physician, and philosopher.

and Eve, the fall of man, and the structure of the universe, which she describes as "egg-shaped." She followed this with a book about the struggle between virtues and vices titled *Liber Vitae Meritorum* (*The Book of the Rewards of Life*). Hildegard's third book was her most ambitious. *Liber Divinorum Operum* (*Book of Divine Works*), finished in 1173, represents ten visions and covers themes of creation and humanity. Hildegard pays close attention to universal feminine spiritual energy throughout this text.

In his bestselling work of popular neuroscience, *The Man Who Mistook His Wife for a Hat*, Oliver Sacks speculates that Hildegard's visions may have been caused by migraine headaches or a brain lesions. Sacks adds, however, that a physiological explanation for Hildegard's visions does not invalidate her spiritual insights. Regardless of their precise origins, Hildegard's visions provided the impetus for a compelling theology and a highly original life's work.

Héloïse

Héloïse was a French nun, writer, and scholar who was fluent in Latin, Greek, and Hebrew. She is best known for her tragic love affair and subsequent epistolary relationship with the brilliant twelfth-century French philosopher and monk Peter Abelard. Though a formidable scholar in her right, Héloïse's correspondence with Abelard is her most enduring literary achievement. First published in Paris in 1616,

ILLUMINATED MANUSCRIPTS

Before the invention of the printing press in 1455, books were written by hand on parchment and often embellished with gold or silver leaf. Decorative textual elements such as oversized opening letters to paragraphs, small illustrations, and marginalia were illuminated in gold. Most illuminated manuscripts were written by monks, but there is evidence that as many as 145 illuminated manuscripts were produced by women. Identifying them all has proved difficult for researchers, but their existence points toward the aesthetic contributions women made despite the restrictions often placed on them by religious orders.

the letters have been in print ever since. Héloïse's and Abelard's love affair was larger than life, and they can be compared with such well-known literary lovers as Romeo and Juliet and Dante and Beatrice.

Héloïse came from a family with some money, but her letters suggest that her family ranked below the nobility. Her most important family connection was a canon (a rank similar to a priest) named Fulbert. Abelard, a fellow canon, had a reputation as a leading Parisian teacher and philosopher. In his letters, Abelard confesses to seducing Héloïse: "and so I yielded to the lusts of the flesh . . . There was in Paris at the time a young girl named Héloïse, the niece of Fulbert." Héloïse and Fulbert lived together,

Shown here is artist Robert Bateman's portrait of Héloïse and Abelard, dating from 1879. This scene of calm courtship presaged a legendary, passionate romance.

and Abelard offered to tutor Héloïse in exchange for board in their house. The two became lovers, and Héloïse soon gave birth to their son Astrolabe. Under pressure from Fulbert, Abelard agreed to marry Héloïse, but he wanted to keep the marriage secret for "career reasons." When Abelard moved Héloïse into a convent, Fulbert and a gang of friends attacked and castrated Abelard as punishment. Abelard then became a monk at the Abbey of St. Denis.

Héloïse and Abelard began exchanging letters after their separation. While the letters reflect on their relationship and the trauma they both endured, Héloïse and Abelard also wrote passionately to each other about philosophy and religion. In what may be considered an early articulation of feminist ideas, Heloise expresses her disdain for marriage, and compares wedlock to prostitution.

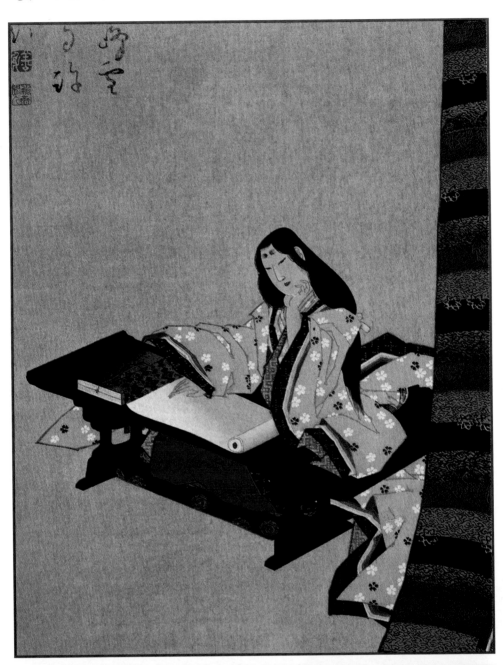

The author Murasaki Shikibu, of ancient Japan's Fujiwara family, is depicted here. Her book *The Tale of Genji* is considered the world's first novel. Here she is represented on a hanging scroll on silk.

She also describes childrearing as a chore rather than a sacred duty: "What man, bent on sacred or philosophical thoughts, could endure the crying of children . . . ? And what woman will be able to bear the constant filth and squalor of babies?" Abelard agreed and published similar sentiments. Although Héloïse is often considered in relation to Abelard, it is clear from her writing that she was a highly original thinker.

Murasaki Shikibu

Murasaki Shikibu was born into the elite Fujiwara family of Japan around the year 976. She was the daughter of a governor, whose family included a line of poets. After the death of her husband, she was brought to royal court based on her reputation as a woman of great learning. Murasaki kept a diary at this time to chronicle the events she witnessed in court, which she criticized for being frivolous. Murasaki wrote most of *The Tale of Genji* while at court. Through the fictional tale of a prince called Genji, Murasaki depicted the events and mores of upper-class society. The book immediately became popular, and has been studied and discussed for over a thousand years. *The Tale of Genji* is considered by many scholars to be the world's first novel.

CHAPTER THREE

RENAISSANCE WOMEN

The Renaissance was a period in European history that began in fourteenth-century Italy. It was characterized by renewed interest in the civilizations of classical Greece and Rome. The status of women during this time was little better than during the Middle Ages. Women were legally subject to their husbands' authority and denied all political rights. Women were primarily relegated to the home and were not permitted to live independently. For woman with philosophical or literary ambitions, convents and similar religious institutions served as essential refuges and cultural centers. These places facilitated the creation of important and lasting literary works by women.

Christine de Pizan

The Italian-French writer Christine de Pizan wrote forty-one works of poetry and prose between 1399 and 1429 and is best known for her books about women. These works can be considered some of the earliest examples of feminist theory in European intellectual history. Her 1399 book, *Epistre au Dieu D'amour,* deals with the status of women in society, offering a cogent historical study of literary representations of women. She followed this with two more feminist texts in 1405, *Le Livre de la Cité des Dames* (*The Book of the City of Ladies*) and *Le Trésor de la Cité des Dames* (*The Treasure of the City of Ladies*).

De Pizan's writing arose from her material and emotional circumstances. At the age of twenty-five, she lost her husband to the bubonic plague, a disease that killed almost a third of the population in Europe. De Pizan's father, who was an astrologist and physician to the king of France, also died relatively young. These deaths caused de Pizan considerable strain, as she was responsible for supporting her two children, her mother, and a niece. She began writing poetry as a way to cope with her husband's death. After gaining the attention of wealthy patrons at court, she was able to support herself and those in her charge by writing. She composed over three hundred ballads and poems, many of which were commissioned by her wealthy new clients.

Christine de Pizan presents a manuscript to Isabel of Bavaria in this vibrant medieval illustration.

With her livelihood secured, de Pizan entered her mature phase of writing. She established herself as a public intellectual by writing about sexism in a book called *The Romance of the Rose* by Jean de Meun. She objected to de Meun's indecent terms for female sexuality, as well as his insinuation that all women were seducers. She also wrote her two most famous books, *The Book of the City of Ladies* and *The Treasure of the City of Ladies*, during this period. The former reversed negative stereotypes about women by constructing an imaginary, female-centric city. An important insight of the book is that maintaining negative impressions of women requires excluding them from public discourse. Her next book took up similar themes while arguing that women's rhetorical skills were important conduits of social good. Her final work was a poem from 1429 about Joan of Arc.

In 1949, the French feminist philosopher Simone de Beauvoir commented that de Pizan was "the first woman [to] take up the pen in defense of her sex." De Beauvoir's endorsement of de Pizan suggests some continuity between de Pizan's ideas and feminism today.

The Italian Humanists: Laura Cereta and Cassandra Fedele

The term "humanism" describes an ethical, educational, and philosophical position that came to prominence in northern Italy in the thirteenth and fourteenth centuries before spreading to the rest of Europe. Humanism valued civic engagement, clear expression, freedom, progress, and rational thought. As the term suggests, humanism focuses on human beings rather than the divine. And it rejected the superstition and dogma that characterized education in the Middle Ages in favor of evidence and human reason. Humanist subjects such as history, philosophy, poetry, and rhetoric are the precursors to what we now call the humanities. This intellectual atmosphere produced a number of remarkable women writers, including Laura Cereta and Cassandra Fedele.

Laura Cereta was born in 1469 to an upper-class family in Brescia, Italy. She was educated in a convent, where she excelled at a variety of subjects. Her studies were twice interrupted when Laura was called home to help her parents with family responsibilities. At age fifteen, she married a businessman named Pietro Serina. Her marriage

This 1869 watercolor by Frederick William Burton is of Cassandra Fedele, a poet and musician from sixteenth-century Venice, Italy.

provided the raw material for some of her early letters in which she discussed her ideal of marriage and proper spousal relations.

Although Cereta died at age thirty, she enjoyed public recognition for her scholarship and writing during her short life. Her eight-two letters, organized in 1488 into a collection called *Epistole Familiares*, provide illuminating insights into her ideas. Her letters speak to women's issues particularly, exploring subjects such as war, politics, friendship, and education from a female perspective. Her candor met with some critical backlash, but she dealt forcefully with these criticisms. She is remembered as an early humanist feminist and foundational figure for women who would take up her lines of thought.

Cassandra Fedele, a contemporary of Laura Cereta's, was a preeminent female humanist scholar of the fifteenth century. Fedele was born in Venice in 1465, and by age twelve she was fluent in Greek and Latin. She was educated in the classics under the supervision of a monk named Gasparino Borro.

In 1487, Fedele delivered a speech titled *Oratio pro Bertucio Lamberto* at a relative's graduation in Padua. The speech praised the arts and sciences, and earned her recognition for her diligent scholarship. Its publication in several Italian cities as well as in Nuremberg, Germany, marked the beginning of a productive but short-lived writing career.

Fedele was most active as a writer between the ages of twenty-two and thirty-three. Her many philosophical and theological letters and orations were collected in a posthumous volume published in Padua in 1636. After her marriage at age thirty-four, Fedele's literary activity dramatically decreased. This was due perhaps to the pressure on married women to focus on private family life instead of public life, although illness and her husband's death may have contributed to the dearth of published material from this period of her life. There is evidence she wrote a late work called *Ordo scientiarum,* but unfortunately this text is now lost. Fedele died in 1558.

BEYOND EUROPE

While Europeans rediscovered classical civilization during the fifteenth and sixteenth centuries, other cultures outside of Europe did not experience the contrast between a dark age and a rebirth. In India, for example, there exists an unbroken tradition of scholarship. Two important Indian women writers emerged around this time: Tallapaka Timmakka and Atukuri Molla. Both women wrote in an Indian language called Telugu. Molla's major work of simple, conversational poetry is known as *Molla bhagavata.*

(continued on the next page)

(continued from the previous page)

Timmakka's major work is a Telugu version of a Sanskrit epic called *Subhadra Kalyanam*, about the marriage of two characters, Arjuna and Subhadra.

In the Islamic world, a prodigious mystical Sufi poet living in Damascus named 'A'isha al-Ba'uniyya wrote a wealth of works. She became one of the few well-known Islamic female poets of this or any subsequent era.

Subhadra is said to be the half sister of Krishna. Carrying passengers Arjuna and Krishna, she is illustrated here driving a chariot away from Dwarka.

Women of the English Renaissance: Catherine Parr and Anne Askew

The Renaissance in England began slightly later than the Italian Renaissance. The beginning of the English Renaissance coincides loosely with the end of the Wars of the Roses in 1485 and the beginning of the Tudor Dynasty. William Shakespeare and Edmund Spenser are the most well-known writers of the English Renaissance. However, a significant amount of writing, including prose, plays, and poetry, was produced by women during this period.

Catherine Parr was queen of England from 1543 to 1547. She was the last of King Henry VIII's six wives and the only one to survive him. Though less known for her writing, Parr was in fact the first woman in England to publish under her own name. The four publications attributed to Parr address the changing role of religion in society and the nature of individual faith during the English Reformation, when the Church of England broke off from the Catholic Church. She also oversaw the education of her three stepchildren: Prince Edward, Princess Mary, and Princess Elizabeth.

Catherine Parr was born in 1512 to Sir Thomas Parr and Maud Green, who both served in the royal household. Parr received an education befitting an aristocratic. She displayed an unusual aptitude for languages. Early on, she became fluent in Latin, Italian, and French, and she learned Spanish after

The order and manner of the burning of *Ann*
John Adams, *Nicholas Belenian*, with certaine of
fitting in Smithfield.

w, *John Lacels,*
ıncell

she ascended to the throne. Parr married Henry VIII in July of 1543, making her Queen of England and Ireland. When Henry left England for a military campaign in France, Parr acted as regent in his place. As such, she influenced government policy, and also restored her stepchildren Mary and Elizabeth to the royal line of succession.

Experts on the English Reformation view Parr's writing in the context of debates about the degree to which an individual's knowledge of scripture was necessary for salvation. Parr's second book The *Lamentation of a Sinner* (1547) expounds on these ideas. Although Parr

This illustration depicts the burning of Anne Askew, John Lascelles, John Adams, and Nicholas Belenian in 1546. Branded a heretic, Anne Askew was tortured in the Tower of London before being burned at the stake.

was nominally a Catholic, she broke from orthodox Catholic doctrine by teaching that faith alone was sufficient justification to pardon a sinner. In this way, she displayed an affinity for emerging strains of Protestantism. Although she wrote three other books, Psalms or Prayers, Prayers or Meditations, and a compilation of Biblical excerpts, *Lamentation* is her most influential work. Parr's life was cut short in 1548 from complications due to childbirth, just six days after her only daughter, Mary Seymour, was born.

Parr's contemporary and friend, the Protestant martyr Anne Askew, adopted a different position on religion. Unlike Parr, who defended traditional religious authority and social hierarchy, Askew put forth an egalitarian vision of spirituality. In addition to her writing on religion, Askew was one of the earliest female English poets. She was also the first woman to ask for a divorce based on religious difference. For this she was branded a heretic and tortured in the Tower of London before being burned at the stake in 1546.

Anne Askew was born in 1521. She was a devoted Protestant and an outspoken critic of transubstantiation, the Catholic belief that the bread and wine offered in the sacrament becomes the body and blood of Jesus Christ. When Askew's older sister died, their father arranged her late sister's fiancé Thomas Kyme to marry Anne instead. Kyme was Catholic, and the marriage ended badly. After Kyme kicked Askew out of their house, she went to London and became a preacher. She was arrested a number of times and was taken to the Tower of London, where she was the only woman to be tortured on the rack.

Askew's book *Examinations* argues for the primacy of personal interpretations of scripture. The book is a vivid, first-person chronicle of her life and the ordeals she suffered for her beliefs. It highlights her aptitude for theological and legal arguments against male authority figures. The English writer and churchman John Bale published and annotated the book after Askew's death, earning her recognition as a Protestant martyr and as a woman who spoke out on religious matters.

CHAPTER FOUR

SENSE, SENSIBILITY, AND THE VINDICATION OF WOMEN (1600–1800)

T he seventeenth century was a turbulent time in England. A civil war raged between the Royalists and the Parliamentarians, who were known as Roundheads because many of them cut their hair short, unlike the Royalists who wore their hair in long curls. The English Civil War culminated with the beheading of King Charles I and the ascent of Oliver Cromwell. By the eighteenth century, England became the dominant colonial power in Europe, eclipsing France and the Netherlands. These events informed the literature of the time.

Aphra Behn

Aphra Behn was the first English woman to earn her living by writing. Occasionally using the pseudonym Astrea, Behn wrote fiction, plays, poetry, and

British painter Mary Beale painted this portrait (oil on canvas) of Aphra Behn. Behn is the earliest female author in England to take up the pen professionally.

translations. Although there is scant biographical information about Behn, her *nom de plume* may have originated during her brief stint as a spy for Charles II in Antwerp, Belgium. Behn's most famous work is a short novel called *Oroonoko: or, the Royal Slave.* It tells the story of an African prince who is tricked into slavery in Surinam, and is partially based on Behn's experiences in the Americas. *Oroonoko* is one of the first modern novels and is still widely studied for its complex characterization and forthright treatment of race and gender.

Unlike most early female authors, Behn was of humble class origins. Her father Bartholomew Johnson probably worked as a barber. Little else is known about Behn's early life. Born in 1640 in Kent, Behn was named Eaffrey Johnson at birth. As a young adult, she traveled to colonial Surinam with her family. This trip informed some elements of *Oroonoko,* but the degree to which the novel is based on actual events is open to dispute. Her father may have died during this journey, but biographers are unsure.

Behn married Johann Behn, and was thereafter known professionally as Mrs. Behn. After her marriage, Behn became a spy during the Second Anglo-Dutch War. The premature death of her husband left Behn in debt, and she probably served time in a debtor's prison. Her literary career was born out of material need. Behn worked as a scribe for the King's Company and the Duke's Company, the two major theatrical companies of the day.

Behn's first literary success was a play called *The Forc'd Marriage* in 1670. Her next play, *The Amorous Prince*, followed in 1671. Her third play, *The Dutch Lover*, was a flop, and Behn disappeared from the theater scene for three years. She reappeared with a tragedy called *Abdelazer* and two successful comic works, *The Rover* and *Love-Letters Between a Nobleman and His Sister*. By 1688, Behn's mature voice as a narrator emerged with *Oroonoko* and another short novel called *The Fair Jilt*.

According to biographer Janet Todd, Behn was, "not so much a woman to be unmasked as an unending combination of masks." However, Behn's lasting literary influence is due more to the psychological complexity and carefully rendered realism of her writing than to her double life as a writer and spy.

Mary Wollstonecraft

There were early feminist writers before Mary Wollstonecraft, but none articulated a feminist vision as fully formed and influential as hers. Mary Wollstonecraft's *A Vindication of the Rights of Woman* (1792) is thought to be the first feminist treatise ever written. The book identifies a lack of equality between the sexes and points toward several historical factors that impede women from achieving their full human potential. These factors include inferior education, a lack of economic

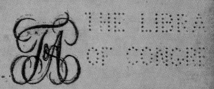

A

VINDICATION

OF THE

RIGHTS OF WOMAN:

WITH

STRICTURES

ON

POLITICAL AND MORAL SUBJECTS.

BY MARY WOLLSTONECRAFT.

THE LIBRA
OF CONGR

PRINTED AT BOSTON,
BY PETER EDES FOR THOMAS AND ANDREWS,
FAUST's Statue, No. 45, Newbury-Street,
MDCCXCII.

Shown here is a rare early manuscript of Mary Wollstonecraft's *A Vindication of the Rights of Woman: With Strictures on Political and Moral Subjects*. The book is a pioneering work of early feminist theory.

independence, and the imposition of limited roles in society.

Wollstonecraft's capacity for incisive analysis arose partially from unhappy early life experiences. Wollstonecraft was born in London in 1759 and grew up with an abusive father. In 1780, her mother died and her father lost a large sum of money in an agricultural venture. This prompted Wollstonecraft and her sister Eliza to leave home. After a short stint working as a governess in Ireland, a job she disliked, Wollstonecraft moved back to London to work with Joseph Johnson on a publication called the *Analytical Review*. Her early contributions to this radical journal laid the groundwork for the revolutionary ideas she later published under her own name.

Wollstonecraft had a daughter with an American named Gilbert Imlay, but true to her belief that marriage represented tyranny, the two did not marry. After this relationship ended, Wollstonecraft began a relationship with the anarchist William Godwin and the couple had a daughter named Mary. The younger Mary went on to write the novel *Frankenstein*. Wollstonecraft died in 1797 from complications due to childbirth.

In addition to *A Vindication of the Rights of Woman*, Wollstonecraft wrote about the French Revolution in *An Historical and Moral View of the Origin and Progress of the French Revolution* (1794) and a successful travel narrative, *Letters Written During a Short Residence in Sweden, Norway and Denmark* (1796).

BLUE STOCKINGS SOCIETY

The Blue Stockings was a name given to the ad-hoc social and literary gatherings for intellectually inclined women during the second half of the eighteenth century in England. This informal movement began around 1750, and although it was never a centrally organized society, the gatherings created a valuable social platform for women. Blue Stockings gatherings provided intellectually-stimulating evenings for women instead of idle pastimes such as playing cards. The gatherings were not limited to women, however. They often included male guest lecturers. One such guest, Benjamin Stillingfleet, allegedly gave the group its name. When he declined an invitation because he lacked appropriate dress, one of the ladies suggested he come wearing only his blue stockings. He did just that, and the name stuck. Prominent women of the Blue Stockings movement included Elizabeth Montague, Elizabeth Carter, Fanny Burney, and Hannah More. More's 1789 poem "The Bas Bleu, or Conversation" is a key document of the movement.

Jane Austen

Jane Austen is among the greatest novelists in the English language. Though she was not as widely read in her own day, her six major novels have gained enormous popularity and critical esteem. Her posthumous ascent to literary canonization began with the publication of *A Memoir of Jane Austen* in 1869, and peaked in the twentieth century with the adaptation of her works for film and television. Her novels such as *Pride and Prejudice* and *Sense and Sensibility* merged romance and realism while astutely commenting on the conditions of life, particularly for women, among the landowning class in late eighteenth-century Britain.

Jane Austen was born in Steventon, Hampshire, England, in December 1775. She came from a large family that valued education. Austen's father George was an Oxford-educated Anglican rector, and her mother Cassandra had ties to the aristocracy. From an early age, Austen and her sister Cassandra were often found reading volumes from their father's large library, and the two put on plays for the entertainment of the family. Jane was sent to boarding school but returned to live at home after a near-fatal bout with typhus and family financial hardship.

Austen's earliest works, written in the last decade of the eighteenth century, were genre parodies. They are now collected in a volume called *Juvenilia*. The first was an epistolary romance called *Love and Freindship* [sic]. Another called *The History of England* cleverly mocks historical writing. The last work of her early phase was a short novel called *Lady Susan*. Critics identify the novel's frank portrayal of an intelligent but manipulative woman as a harbinger of themes to come from the budding novelist.

Shown here is the front cover of an 1883 edition of Jane Austen's beloved novel *Pride and Prejudice*, published by George Routledge & Sons.

Austen began publishing her work after her father's death in 1805. Her six mature novels, *Sense and Sensibility, Pride and Prejudice, Northanger Abbey, Mansfield Park, Emma,* and *Persuasion*, were published between 1811 and 1819. Austen published all of her novels anonymously, which was a common practice at the time for women authors. Her novels from this time period examine the British social system among the land-owning class and highlight women's dependence on marriage to maintain social standing and economic security. Due to her outstanding wit, use of irony, and cutting social commentary, scholars have long regarded her as an important and transitional literary figure for nineteenth-century realism. Although Austen's novels were commercial and critical successes, she experienced little fame during her lifetime. All of her major novels sold out of their first printings. Her novels have been in print ever since. Austen fell ill and died in 1817.

Spanish and Chilean Women Writers

English literature was not the only source for women's writing in the eighteenth century. In Spain, a few women earned advanced degrees and published in the fields of math and science. It was highly unusual for women to write on these subjects at the time.

Cultural biases against women becoming scientists or mathematicians remain strong today. The women who overcame such biases centuries ago are exceptional when viewed in this light.

María Andrea Casamayor, born in 1700 in Zaragoza, Spain, was an accomplished author, mathematician, and scientist. She published two works in her lifetime, both of which entered the educational curricula. *Tirocinio Aritmético* was published in 1738, and her second book *El Para sí Solo* followed shortly thereafter. Casamayor's texts are some of the very few scientific works published by Spanish women during this time period.

Born in 1768, María Pascuala Caro Sureda studied at the University of Valencia, earning her doctorate in 1779. Her book on physics and mathematics titled *Ensayo de Historia, Física y Matemáticas* was published in 1781. She entered a convent in 1789 and was known thereafter for her mystical poems.

Spanish language writing flourished in the New World during the eighteenth century as well. In colonial Chile, two women rose to prominence for their writing. Tadea de San Joaquin, a Carmelite nun, was born in 1750 in Santiago, Chile, to an educated family. In 1783, her convent was struck by severe flooding. She wrote a 516-verse poem about the experience. This ambitious work, influenced by Baroque and epic poetry, made Tadea de San Joaquin the first known Chilean female poet. She continued to write poems until her death in 1827.

The Iglesia-Convento de Santa Teresa, in Ávila, Spain, is part of the Carmelite order. It was finished in 1636.

Josefa de los Dolores Peña y Lillo Barbosa was another Chilean woman writer and a nun of the Dominican Order. Like many nuns in the New World, her writing consists mainly of letters. A 2008 critical edition of her work titled *Epistolary of Sister Dolores Peña y Lillo (Chile, 1763–1769)* collects sixty-five of her letters.

AIN'T I A NINETEENTH-CENTURY WOMAN?

The nineteenth century is marked by cultural, economic, and industrial changes around the world. Rapidly expanding empires and new technologies like the steamship, the railroad, and the telegraph allowed literary movements to spread in an unprecedented manner. Realism, one of the most influential literary movements, grew out of this time. As a style, realism is concerned with representing everyday reality. Although it began in Britain and France, realism soon spread throughout the world. Because people from different cultures often experience and represent reality in their own way, literary realism takes on many forms.

Emily Dickinson and Rebecca Harding Davis in the United States, Joauquim Maria Machado de Assis in Brazil, Higuchi Ichiyo from Japan, and other women writers of the nineteenth century made lasting contributions to world literature by inventing new literary techniques, altering literary conventions, and experimenting with different styles of writing. Women's suffrage movements and first-wave feminism gained international momentum during the nineteenth century.

Women of the American Renaissance

The American Renaissance in literature of the nineteenth century is usually synonymous with male writers and thinkers such as Ralph Waldo Emerson, Henry David Thoreau, Herman Melville, and Nathanial Hawthorne. However, this was a time of extraordinary diversity in America. Slave and European immigrant populations were rapidly growing, giving rise to a host of different literary, philosophical, and political movements, such as the antislavery movement known as abolitionism. Literary traditions such as transcendentalism, romanticism, and realism were all in formation. Women writers gained a wider audience in America during this time, and many women contributed to political and intellectual discourse.

Abolitionist Literature

Abolitionists were opponents of slavery in the United States. Many key abolitionists were women, some of whom were formerly enslaved. Sojourner Truth is one of the most famous female abolitionists. A former slave, she gave the rousing speech "Ain't I a Woman?" to audiences at the Women's Convention in Akron, Ohio, in 1851. The short speech criticized common arguments against rights for women and black people: "Then they talk about this thing in the head; what's this they call it? [member of audience whispers, "intellect"] That's it, honey. What's that got to do with women's rights or negroes' rights? If my cup won't hold but a pint, and yours holds a quart, wouldn't you be mean not to let me have my little half measure full?"

Slave narratives were very popular during the nineteenth century, particularly Frederick Douglass's 1845 autobiography *Narrative of the Life of Frederick Douglass, an American Slave*. An escaped slave named Harriet Jacobs published *Incidents in the Life of a Slave Girl* under the pseudonym Linda Brent in 1861. Lydia Maria Child, a white abolitionist and women's rights activist, helped Jacobs to edit and publish the book. Although Child is probably best known for her poem "Over the River and Through the Wood," she also wrote *An Appeal in Favor of That Class of Americans Called Africans*, which argued that slaves should be freed immediately and that slave owners should not be compensated for their losses.

The most influential novel from the abolitionist movement is Harried Beecher Stowe's *Uncle Tom's Cabin*, published in 1852. Stowe was born in Litchfield, Connecticut, in 1811 to a Calvinist family. She was morally outraged by slavery. After the Fugitive Slave Law of 1850, which required all escaped slaves

This poster is an advertisement for Harriet Beecher Stowe's towering abolitionist novel, *Uncle Tom's Cabin*. The book was already a literary sensation by the time this poster was printed in 1859.

to be returned to their masters, Stowe felt that no person could remain quiet about the evils of slavery. *Uncle Tom's Cabin* depicted the horrors of slavery and was the bestselling novel of the nineteenth century, making Stowe famous during her lifetime. When Stowe met President Abraham Lincoln, he famously called her "the little woman who started this great war." The first widely read political novel in the United States, *Uncle Tom's Cabin* greatly influenced the genre of the protest novel and American literature in general. Though the novel has been read as a contribution to feminist theory because of its critique of the patriarchal nature of slavery, many scholars and readers today criticize the book for what they view as its racist depictions of its black characters, particularly Uncle Tom, who passively accepts his fate and dies at the end of the novel. During the 1960s, several black activists and writers took issue with the novel, arguing that it represented crude stereotypes and that its author was condescending toward black people. Nevertheless, *Uncle Tom's Cabin* remains a vital document in the history of American slavery and racism and it is widely taught in American literature courses today.

The Poetry of Emily Dickinson

Born in 1830 to a prominent family in Amherst, Massachusetts, Emily Dickinson is one of the best-known American poets. Dickinson lived a life of quiet isolation and confinement as a young adult

This portrait shows the reclusive poet Emily Dickinson circa 1850. Her innovative verse has earned her work a prominent place among the best-known American poetry of any era.

until her death in 1888. By the end of her life, she was well known throughout the town as the strange "woman in white." Reclusive and withdrawn, she was a private person who never left her father's house. She published only ten poems during her lifetime, all anonymously. Dickinson begged for her letters and numerous hand-made volumes of poetry to be destroyed after her death. Her relatives did not honor this wish, however, and published the poems.

Dickinson's poetry captured the hearts and minds of readers and scholars alike with its unusual use of slant rhyme, startling imagery, blank or broken meter, and innovative free verse. Her poems are known for their brevity, throwing readers immediately into the heart of the poem. While the poems contemplate common themes such as death, God, love, nature, and religious faith, they do so with such striking imagery and originality that they in many ways have more in common with the experimental poetry that came a century later. Her poems often treat complex or grand subjects as ordinary events. The speaker in "I Heard a Fly Buzz" describes the moment of death not as a dramatic departure from the earthly realm but as a tedious event bound up in everyday life, symbolized by the distraction of a buzz from a common housefly during death. Dickinson was highly nonconformist, refused religious dogma, and dropped out of college. Her poem "I'm Nobody! Who are You?" questions the value of a social status: "How dreary— to be Somebody! / How public—like a Frog— / To tell one's name the livelong June / To an admiring

Bog!" Dickinson's inventiveness was fostered by the freedom provided by privacy and anonymity. Her poems transformed the literary landscape.

British Literature

The nineteenth century was an era of great change everywhere, and it was particularly so for women in Britain. Women's rights to vote, to own property, and to control their bodies were all intensely debated topics and women sought to influence the discussions concerning their lives. Writing was a platform for women to express their thoughts and to reach an audience beyond their private spheres of influence. Moreover, an expanding variety of publications, from pamphlets and penny presses to more expensive bound editions, gave the growing number of professional female authors many publishing options.

Women of the nineteenth century had significant barriers to overcome, however. Oxford and Cambridge, the major universities in England, did not become coeducational until the 1860s and 1870s, and before this women were not allowed to pursue higher education in England. Women had to contend with the common notion that a woman's place is in the home. Writing was a way for women to fight oppressive practices and ideologies and, for some, to secure economic independence. The literary marketplace grew during the Victorian era, and a number of female

PRESCRIPTIVE LITERATURE

Behavioral tracts, domestic manuals, and etiquette books were popular in the nineteenth century, and women wrote many of these "prescriptive" texts. Popular etiquette books instructed women on the proper way to dress, write letters, and serve tea. Some of these books were resolutely anti-feminist, such as Eliza Lynn Linton's 1822 collection of essays, *Girl of the Period*. Linton argues that women have no place in politics or pursuing public renown, and she railed against the rising "New Woman," a late-nineteenth-century feminist term that describes women's increased control over their social, economic, and personal lives. Linton argues that women and men have distinct natures that render them unsuitable for some tasks and adept at others.

authors such as Elizabeth Gaskell, Mary Braddon, and Margaret Oliphant enjoyed brief popularity. A few female authors, including the novelists George Eliot and Charlotte Brontë, created works that transcended their moment and are widely read and studied today.

Charlotte Brontë and George Eliot

Charlotte Brontë's 1847 novel, *Jane Eyre,* and George Eliot's 1871 novel, *Middlemarch,* are among the most revered works of English literature. Both books consistently appear on lists of the greatest novels of all time in any language, further supporting the innovative role female authors played in literature.

Charlotte Brontë was born in 1816 to a family that included her famous literary sisters Emily and Anne. The specter of death haunted the family. Brontë lost her mother and two older siblings early in life. Raised in a strict Anglican tradition by her father and religious aunt, Brontë was homeschooled after an unhappy stint in boarding school. Inspired by a gift of tin soldiers from her father, Brontë began composing stories early in her life. Her juvenile tales involved her imagined heroes, Charles and Arthur Wellesley, and employed mature themes such as romance and sexual politics. In her writing, Brontë represented artists and poets as slightly morally degenerate.

With her sisters Emily and Anne, Brontë published a collection of poems under the pseudonym Currer Bell. Although the book sold poorly, it opened the doors for her 1847 novel *Jane Eyre* to become popular. *Jane Eyre*'s eponymous protagonist is an orphan and governess to the ward of Mr. Rochester. Jane Eyre and Mr. Rochester fall in love, but Jane leaves him when she discovers that he is married and keeps his mad wife locked away in the attic. The novel's carefully paced plot, romance, and satiric reworking of gothic themes earned it a loyal following. Her subsequent novels *Shirley* and *Villette* were also well received. Some modern critics such as Lucy Hughes-Hallett of *The Telegraph* consider *Villette* to be Brontë's greatest novel.

"MARRY? I DON'T WANT TO MARRY, AND NEVER
SHALL MARRY."

This illustration is taken from an illustrated edition of *Jane Eyre*, by Charlotte Brontë. The caption refers to the novel's marriage plot, which is juxtaposed against characteristics of the gothic literary tradition.

George Eliot was a pseudonym used by Mary Ann Evans, born in 1819 in Warwickshire. When her mother died in 1836, Eliot quit school to help her father in Coventry. After her father's death in 1849, she traveled abroad before finally settling in London, where she soon became a contributor to a journal of radical philosophy called *Westminster Review*. It was in this intellectual circle that Eliot met George Henry Lewes, a married man with whom Eliot was romantically involved and cohabitated with for the next twenty-four years until his death.

Eliot's earliest literary works were essays and translations, including an English-language version of Ludwig Feuerbach's classic work of theology *Essence of Christianity*. She followed this with a collection of stories titled *Scenes of Clerical Life* (1858), which marked the first appearance of her pen name. In her next two novels, *Adam Bede* (1859), and *The Mill on the Floss* (1860), Eliot honed the blend of humor, moral sensitivity, and intense psychological realism, that would become her hallmark as an author.

Eliot's undisputed masterpiece, *Middlemarch* (1871), was originally published in eight installments. The novel chronicles the interlocking lives of people living in Middlemarch, a fictional midlands town. It is considered by many to be among the greatest novel in the English language. Eliot followed this with *Daniel Deronda* (1876), an unusual British novel in that it features Jewish protagonists. Eliot died in 1880 at age sixty-one, shortly after she married her friend John Walter Cross.

MADWOMEN IN ATTICS

The Madwoman in the Attic: The Woman Writer and the Nineteenth-Century Literary Imagination is an important work of feminist literary criticism published in 1979 by Sandra Gilbert and Susan Gubar. The book's title alludes to the madwoman locked in the attic in Charlotte Brontë's novel *Jane Eyre*. Gilbert and Gubar argue that nineteenth-century women writers used similar themes of confinement to convey the experiences of women in patriarchal societies. The madwoman in the attack symbolizes women's rage at their predicament. One of the central insights of the book is that women writers tended to conform to the angel/monster trope in their characterizations of women. That is, representations of women were frequently limited to either angelic or monstrous figures. Gilbert and Gubar urged women to break out of these constraints in their writing.

Poetry

The nineteenth century was something of a golden age for female poets in Britain. Most prominent among these poets were Elizabeth Barrett Browning and Christina Rossetti. Elizabeth Barrett Browning's first two collections, *The Seraphim and Other Poems* (1838) and *Poems* (1844), established her reputation and gained the attention of famous poet Robert Browning, whom she later married. Her two best-known works, the collection *Sonnets from the Portuguese* and the epic poem *Aurora Leigh*, were written in Italy and influenced by Browning's interest in Italian politics.

Rossetti's most famous poem is called "Goblin Market," a tale of two sisters who encounter these supernatural creatures. The poem can be read as an allegory of the fallen woman trope and also a feminist comment on Victorian gender roles.

CHAPTER SIX

TWENTIETH-CENTURY AND CONTEMPORARY FEMALE WRITERS

The beginning of the twentieth century saw cultural, economic, and technological transformations like never before in Europe and North America that entailed a full modernization of human experience. The first half of the century gave rise to a world in crisis, with two world wars, the Russian Revolution, the Great Depression, and the Holocaust. These upheavals are reflected in the form and content of literature of the period. The second half of the twentieth century was marked by a postwar boom alongside important cultural changes, with the feminist and civil rights movements gaining momentum.

MODERNISM AND THE HARLEM RENAISSANCE

Modernism is perhaps the most well-known literary and artistic movement of the twentieth century. Modernism peaked between the two world wars and ended roughly in 1945. Modernism began in England and grew out of the Bloomsbury group, a group of artists, intellectuals, and writers that included Virginia Woolf and her sister, the painter Vanessa Bell. Modernism's artistic program was to "make it new," and indeed the movement ushered in radical changes in the form, style, and content of all mediums. Many modernist novels used stream of consciousness, paintings were abstract, and poems like T. S. Eliot's "The Waste Land" spoke to a chaotic world torn by war.

The Harlem Renaissance was a social and artistic movement led by black writers, artists, and intellectuals centered primarily in the Harlem neighborhood of New York City in the 1920s. The Harlem Renaissance is often closely associated with modernism. Zora Neale Hurston is the best-known female writer of the Harlem Renaissance. Her most influential work, *Their Eyes Were Watching God* (1937), describes the experiences of a rural all-black southern community and the particular struggles of black females. Another important Harlem Renaissance novelist, Nella Larsen wrote about the experience of gendered racial oppression in the cities of America and Europe in her novel *Quicksand*.

Virginia Woolf

Born in 1882, the British author Virginia Woolf is one of the greatest modernist novelists. Woolf was a dedicated feminist who examined the unfair situation of women in society, the restrictions of gender identity, and the difficulties women writers faced in particular. Her famous work of nonfiction *A Room of One's Own* (1929) deals explicitly with the inequality women have faced under patriarchy. It is renowned for its scathing critique of male-dominated society where women are often objectified. The book is a model of a feminine literary history and remains a hugely influential work for literary and feminist theorists.

Woolf's fiction is notable for its impressionistic narratives, symbolic themes, and unconventional shifts in perspective, plot, structure, and temporality. Her most well-known novels are *Jacob's Room* (1922), *Mrs. Dalloway* (1925), *To the Lighthouse* (1927), and *The Waves* (1931). All of her works consider questions about women's equality in marriage and the arts.

Jean Rhys

Although Jean Rhys is considered a British writer, she was born in 1890 in British colonial Dominica, where she grew up. And much of her work contains West Indian imagery. She left Dominica and traveled to London at age sixteen, spending time thereafter in Europe and England. She lived an impoverished but

Pearl Freedman took this 1921 photograph of author Jean Rhys. Rhys's incisive, melancholy novels did not reach a broad readership until very late in her life.

storied life as an actress, chorus girl, nanny, recluse, drunk, and, above all, author. Her first husband was a French con artist. Rhys had to earn her own living when he was imprisoned. Rhys used the diaries she kept during her time in England as the basis for her 1934 novel *Voyage in the Dark*. Her first novel *Postures* (1928) was based on her relationship with her mentor, the famous modernist author and critic Ford Maddox Ford, with whom she also had an affair. Her other early novels, *After Leaving Mr. Mackenzie* (1931) and *Good Morning, Midnight* (1939), describe cosmopolitan and bohemian protagonists who reject the normal roles for women of the period. They are a poignant commentary on the plight of woman within patriarchal society. Rhys's protagonists refuse to marry up. They drink, cry, and fail at life, but they have integrity. Rhys's writing skillfully criticizes the British class system with humor and pathos. Though her books were critically successful, Rhys struggled financially and emotionally throughout her life. She achieved success late in life with her most renowned novel, *Wide Sargasso Sea* (1966), which tells the story of the nameless madwoman in the attic from Charlotte Brontë's novel *Jane Eyre*.

Gertrude Stein

Novelist, poet, playwright, and famous for her art collection and Paris salon, Gertrude Stein was an American who spent most of her life as an

Very few people are able to pose in front of a portrait by Picasso, but Gertrude Stein was not most people. This painting of the revered author, critic, and salon host was completed in 1906.

expatriate in Paris. Stein was a key player in the modernist art movement. Along with her lifelong companion and secretary, Alice B. Toklas, Stein held one of the most important literary salons in Paris. The major artists and writers of the time met there, including Ernest Hemingway, Henri Matisse, Pablo Picasso, and Ezra Pound. Stein's relationships with artists enabled her to amass a large collection of modernist art, which she and her brother Leo exhibited for the public.

Stein's literary work is often considered secondary to her large personality. Yet her writing, like much of modernist painting and literature, broke with past conventions in order to create the new. Her 1909 book, *Three Lives*, contains three tales depicting the lives of three radically different women. The book's nonlinear narrative represents the inner and outer realities of its characters. In *Tender Buttons* (1912), Stein pushes the bounds of literary convention by including passages of automatic writing and unusual grammar. It reads like a verbal collage. Stein had much more success with *The Autobiography of Alice B. Toklas* (1933), a memoir of her life in the art world of Paris between the world wars, told from the perspective of Stein's lover and companion, Alice.

Joan Didion

Joan Didion is an American novelist, essayist, memoirist, and screenwriter. She has enjoyed continual critical and commercial success since the 1960s. Her first journalism job was for the magazine *Vogue*, where she began as a copywriter and worked her way up to associate features editor during her seven-year tenure. Didion wrote and published her first novel *Run River* in 1963. Her second, and perhaps best-known, novel, *Play It as It Lays,* was published in 1970. She returned to her home state of California and published her first work of nonfiction, *Slouching Towards Bethlehem*, in 1968. It was a best-selling collection of essays about her experiences in California.

Didion's works established her reputation as an important commentator on American culture and society. Didion's nonfiction essays and reportage work reflect the New Journalism movement. While based on fact, New Journalism has a narrative structure that gives the reader a sense of the author's viewpoints and allows much more creative freedom than standard journalism. Didion is always present in her writing. Didion's other well-known books published in this style include *The White Album* (1979) and *South and West: From a Notebook* (2017). In 2005, Didion was awarded the National Book Award for her touching memoir on death, grief, and mortality, *The Year of Magical Thinking*. The book is based on her life after the sudden death of her husband and literary partner, Gregory Dunne. Her only daughter, Quintana Roo Dunne, died in 2004, and Didion wrote a second memoir on grief and coping with loss called *Blue Nights* (2011). Didion is a master of both investigative journalism and memoir writing.

Toni Morrison

Toni Morrison is a bestselling African American novelist, children's writer, literary critic, poet, and professor emerita of literature at Princeton University. She has been awarded a National Book Award, a Pulitzer Prize, and the Nobel Prize in Literature. Morrison addresses themes of race, class, gender, and American slavery in her work. Morrison graduated from the historically black college Howard University in 1953. She worked for Random House publishing in New York City in the mid-1960s, where she helped bring black authors to the attention of the mainstream by editing and publishing their works.

Morrison published her first novel, *The Bluest Eye*, when she was thirty-nine years old. Like many first novels, it did not reach a wide audience. Yet Morrison soon went on to gather national critical fame with her second and third novels, *Sula* (1973) and *Song of Solomon* (1977). Her most famous and celebrated novel, *Beloved* (1987), tells the story of an escaped slave who chooses to kill her daughter rather than allow her to be recaptured and subjected to the horrors of slavery.

Toni Morrison reads here from her 1977 novel *Song of Solomon*, about an African American man named Macon "Milkman" Dead III.

Agatha Christie

Agatha Christie is best known for her sixty-six mystery novels featuring the fictional detectives Miss Marple and Hercule Poirot. Christie also wrote short stories, plays, and romances under the pseudonym Mary Westmacott. Numerous film adaptations of Agatha Christie's mysteries contributed to her work's lasting popularity. The most recent is the 2017 film *Murder on the Orient Express*, directed by Kenneth Branagh. Agatha Christie is the best-selling author of all time, having sold a staggering two billion copies of her books worldwide.

Christie was born Agatha May Clarissa Miller in 1890 to a British mother and an American father in Devon, England. Her upper-class upbringing was happy, despite her somewhat solitary nature. Christie was educated at home by tutors. She learned music, and was especially fond of her many pets. She married Archie Christie when she was twenty-four years old. Inspired by Sir Arthur Conan Doyle's popular Sherlock Holmes stories, Christie worked on her first detective novel starring Hercule Poirot, *The Mysterious Affair at Styles*, while her husband served in World War I. She completed the novel in 1916, and although it was rejected at first, it was eventually accepted by a publishing house called The Bodly Head. Her second and third novels earned her a small income. Christie's marriage to Archie soon dissolved. In 1930 she married again,

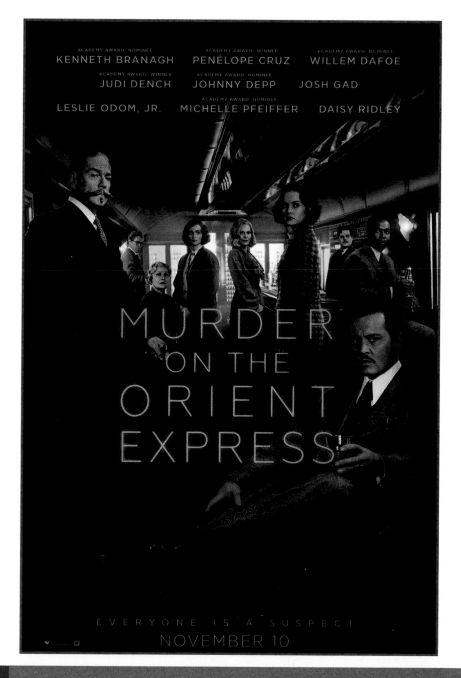

This poster advertises the 2017 remake of *Murder on the Orient Express*, directed by Kenneth Branagh, who also stars in the film as Hercule Poirot. Agatha Christie's novel was first adapted for film in 1974.

this time to an archeologist named Max Mallowan. That same year she wrote *Murder at the Vicarage*, the novel that introduced the world to the beloved fictional detective Miss Jane Marple. Her work has been translated into over one hundred languages, and in 1971, Agatha Christie became a Dame of the British Empire.

MAGICAL REALISM AND ISABEL ALLENDE

Magical realism as a genre has no absolute stylistic boundaries. In fiction, works of magical realism juxtapose supernatural, mythic, or fantastical elements with otherwise mundane settings and events. Although magical realism appears in many literatures around the world, it is usually associated with the Spanish and Latin American literary traditions. Isabel Allende is one of the most prominent female writers who use magical realism in her work.

A Chilean writer, Allende is an innovative magical realist and one of the first female writers from Latin America to see international success. Allende was born in 1942 in Peru, where her father worked in the Chilean embassy. Her uncle was Chilean president Salvador Allende. After he was assassinated in 1973, Allende fled to Venezuela. She published her first novel, *The House of Spirits,* in 1982. The book began as a letter to her terminally ill grandfather. The novel made her reputation. Allende's work mixes elements of magical realism with portrayals of South American politics. In 1996, she founded the Isabel Allende Foundation, a nonprofit organization that supports a range of issues pertaining to women in Chile and the San Francisco Bay Area.

Chilean author Isabel Allende is shown here autographing books at the Miami Book Fair in 2017. Her writing weaves magical realism with political themes.

Young Adult Fiction: S. E. Hinton, Madeleine L'Engle, and Judy Blume

Young adult fiction is marked by its emotional intensity, and usually deals with issues that are relevant to teenagers, including bullying, drugs, family, and sexuality. YA fiction encompasses several genres, such as fantasy, romance, and science fiction. S. E. Hinton, Madeleine L'Engle, and Judy Blume are some of the most influential and successful authors of YA fiction.

S. E. Hinton was born Susan Eloise in Tulsa, Oklahoma, in 1950. She started writing when she was young and her early stories were mostly about cowboys and horses. S. E. Hinton almost singlehandedly pioneered YA fiction with her 1967 novel *The Outsiders*. *The Outsiders* is about a gang rivalry between lower-class Greasers and the affluent Socs. It contains realism that Hinton felt was missing from fiction written for teenagers. Her subsequent novels *Rumble Fish* (1975) and *Tex* (1979) were also bestsellers.

Madeleine L'Engle was born in New York City in 1918. After attending boarding school in Switzerland, she earned her bachelor's degree in English from Smith College in 1941. Four years later she published her first novel, *A Small Rain*. In 1949, she published her first book for young readers, *And Both Were Young*. L'Engle is best known for her 1962 novel *A Wrinkle in Time*, which

Oklahoma native S. E. Hinton is shown here celebrating the fiftieth anniversary of her book *The Outsiders*. The book paved the way for the large young adult literary market of today.

she says was written for her own children. She drew inspiration for the novel from Shakespeare's works and Einstein's theory of relativity. A 2018 film adaptation of the novel directed by Ava DuVernay starred Oprah, Reese Witherspoon, and Mindy Kaling among others.

Judy Blume's 1970s novels such as *Blubber, Tales of a Fourth Grade Nothing*, and *Are You There God? It's Me, Margaret* have been read and cherished by countless children, usually on the cusp of adolescence, and adults. Born Judith Sussman in Elizabeth, New Jersey, Blume married lawyer John Blume in 1959 and earned a bachelor's degree in education from New York University in 1961. About a decade later she published her first book, *The One in the Middle Is the Green Kangaroo*. She wrote prolifically throughout the 1970s, publishing thirteen of her most widely read books. Her work has been translated into more than thirty languages, and she has sold over eighty-two million books. Her work has been both praised and criticized for its frank treatment of sexuality, and her books have occasionally been banned from schools and libraries.

3100 BCE Writing is first devised in ancient Mesopotamia, the area that is now Iraq.

2300 BCE Enheduanna's forty-two "Sumerian Temple Hymns" becomes the earliest known text attributed to an individual author. Thus, the world's first author is female.

660 BCE Lady Xu Mu is the first recorded female poet in Chinese history.

Circa 600–570 BCE Sappho writes about 10,000 lines of poetry on her native island of Lesbos, Greece. Of these lines, only about 650 survived.

130 BCE Roman poet Julia Balbilla inscribes four epigrams known as the "epigrammata" on the statue of Memnon in Egypt.

1021 Japanese writer Murasaki Shikibu publishes *The Tale of Genji*. This book is considered to be the first modern novel.

1115 French abbess Héloïse and philosopher Peter Abelard meet. Abelard would become her lover and a longtime letter-writing partner.

1142 Hildegard of Bingen begins her first book, *Scivias,* a theological text based on her mystical visions.

1405 Italian-French writer Christine de Pizan publishes her two best-known works, *The Book of the City of Ladies* and *The Treasure of the City of Ladies*.

TIMELINE

1547 Catherine Parr publishes *The Lamentation of a Sinner* to great success.

1670 Aphra Behn is employed as a playwright by the King's Company and Duke's Company, making her the first professional female writer in England.

1792 Mary Wollstonecraft publishes *A Vindication of the Rights of Woman,* a pioneering work that is perhaps the earliest example of feminist theory.

1811 Jane Austen draws from her notebooks to begin publishing her six major novels.

1847 Charlotte Brontë publishes *Jane Eyre* under the pseudonym Currer Bell.

1852 Harriet Beecher Stowe publishes *Uncle Tom's Cabin*, the most influential novel of the abolitionist movement.

1871 George Eliot (legal name Mary Ann Evans) publishes *Middlemarch*, one of the greatest novels in the English language.

1929 Virginia Woolf publishes *A Room of One's Own*, in which she argues that more women will produce literature when women have the material conditions to do so.

1930 Agatha Christie writes *Murder at the Vicarage*, the novel that introduces the world to her fictional detective, Miss Marple.

1937 Zora Neale Hurston publishes *Their Eyes Were Watching God*.

1967 S. E. Hinton publishes *The Outsiders*, a foundational novel of young adult fiction.

1993 Toni Morrison wins the Nobel Prize in Literature.
2005 Joan Didion wins the National Book Award
for her memoir on death, grief, and mortality,
The Year of Magical Thinking.

GLOSSARY

canon Literary texts deemed important or essential. The canon, canonization, and canonicity are all evolving and often contested concepts.

cuneiform Meaning "wedge-shaped," cuneiform is a system of writing developed by the Sumerians that used a stylus and clay tablets.

discourse Written or spoken communication or debate.

epic poetry A stylized, lengthy narrative poem about a hero.

feminism Social theory championing human equality and the overturning of oppressive social and political structures. Feminism identifies sexism as a primary cause of inequality and oppression.

gender roles Societal norms of acceptable behavior for men and women.

hierarchy A ranked system of social organization.

humanism A Renaissance cultural movement that placed importance on human experience and thought rather than religious dogma or arbitrary laws.

illuminated manuscript A manuscript style originating in the Middle Ages in which letters and marginalia are decorated with gold, silver leaf, or powder.

manuscript While this term literally means "written by hand," it can include any form of writing before it is published.

marginalia Notes made in the margins of a book.

papyrus Writing surface similar to paper derived from the pith of the papyrus plant.

parchment Writing material made from the hides of animals.

patriarchy A system by which males head the family unit and determine family names. Can also mean systematic and institutionalized male dominance and privilege.

suffrage The right to vote.

verse Metered language that often but not necessarily rhymes. Verse can refer to individual lines of poetry or a full poem.

waves Periods and evolutions within feminist thought, as in "second-wave feminism of the 1960s."

FOR MORE INFORMATION

Canadian Authors Association
6 West Street N, Suite 203
Orillia, ON L3V 5B8
Canada
(705) 325-3926
Website: https://canadianauthors.org/national
Facebook: @canadianauthorsassociation
Twitter: @canauthors
The Canadian Authors Association provides writers
with a wide variety of programs, services, and
resources to help them develop their skills in both
the craft and the business of writing, enhance
their ability to earn a living as a writer, and have
access to a Canada-wide network of writers and
publishing industry professionals.

Canadian Women's Foundation
133 Richmond Street W, Suite 504
Toronto, ON M5H 2L3
Canada
(416) 365-1444
Website: http://www.canadianwomen.org
Facebook: @CanadianWomensFoundation
Twitter: @cdnwomenfdn
The Canadian Women's Foundation is proudly unique.

They are Canada's only national foundation dedicated to giving women and girls in Canada a chance for a better life.

Harriet Beecher Stowe Center
77 Forest Street
Hartford, CT 06105
(860) 522-9258
Website: https://www.harrietbeecherstowecenter.org
Facebook: @HarrietBeecherStowe
Twitter: @HBStoweCenter
The Harriet Beecher Stowe Center offers tours of her preserved home in Hartford, Connecticut. The museum discusses slavery and the role of women in Stowe's work and how these important social issues still resonate today.

International Women's Writing Guild (IWWG)
5 Penn Plaza, 19th Floor, PMB# 19059
New York, NY 10001
(917) 720-6959
Website: http://www.iwwg.org
Facebook: @InternationalWomensWritingGuild
Founded in 1976 by Hannelore Hahn, the International Women's Writing Guild is a nonprofit network for the personal and professional empowerment of women through writing.

Jane Austen's House Museum
Chawton, Alton
Hampshire, GU34 1SD
England
Website: https://www.jane-austens-house-museum
    .org.uk
Jane Austen lived and wrote in this house for the last
    eight years of her life. The museum includes many
    of her personal effects and letters that she wrote.

National Organization for Women (NOW)
1100 H Street NW, Suite 300
Washington, DC 20005
(202) 628-8669
Website: https://now.org
Facebook and Twitter: @NationalNOW
As the grassroots arm of the women's movement,
    the National Organization for Women is dedicated
    to its multi-issue and multi-strategy approach to
    women's rights. Founded in 1966, it is the largest
    organization of feminist grassroots activists in the
    United States.

Women's Fiction Writers Association
Website: http://womensfictionwriters.org
Facebook: @WFWritersAssociation
Twitter: @WF_Writers
The Women's Fiction Writers Association began in
    2013 as an inclusive organization of writers of
    fiction in which the main character's emotional
    journey is of paramount importance.

Women's National Book Association (WNBA)
PO Box 237, FDR Station
New York, NY 10150
(866) 610- 9622
Website: http://www.wnba-books.org
The WNBA's founding idea—that books have power and
    that those involved in their creation gain strength
    from joining forces—reaches across the decades to
    now serve members in chapters across the country
    and network members in between.

FOR FURTHER READING

Adams, Tracey. *Christine de Pizan and the Fight for France.* University Park, PA: The Pennsylvania State University Press, 2018.

Adkins, Lesley, and Roy Adkins. *Jane Austen's England: Daily Life in the Georgian and Regency Period.* New York, NY: Penguin Books, 2014.

Al-Samman, Hamadi. *Anxiety of Erasure: Trauma, Authorship, and the Diaspora in Arab Women's Writings* (Gender, Culture, and Politics in the Middle East). Syracuse, NY: Syracuse University Press, 2015.

DiBattista, Maria, and Deborah Epstein Nord. *At Home in the World: Women Writers and Public Life, from Austen to the Present*. Princeton, NJ: Princeton University Press, 2017.

Dreyer, Elizabeth A. *Accidental Theologians: Four Women Who Shaped Christianity*. Cincinnati, OH: Franciscan Media, 2014.

Fong, Grace S. *Herself an Author: Gender, Agency, and Writing in Late Imperial China*. Honolulu, HI: University of Hawaii Press, 2016.

Freeman, Philip. *Searching for Sappho: The Lost Songs and World of the First Woman Poet*. New York, NY: W.W. Norton & Company, Inc., 2017.

Gates Jr., Henry Louis, ed. *The Portable Nineteenth Century African American Women Writers.* New York, NY: Penguin Books, 2017.

Godwin, William. *Memoirs of the Author of* A
      Vindication of the Rights of Woman. New York, NY:
      Rare Books Club, 2013.
Looser, Devoney. *The Cambridge Companion
      to Women's Writing in the Romantic Period*
      (Cambridge Companions to Literature). New York,
      NY: Cambridge University Press, 2015.

BIBLIOGRAPHY

Abelard, Peter. *The Letters of Abelard and Heloise.*
   New York, NY: 2003.

Chang, Kang-i Sun, and Haun Saussy, eds. *Women
   Writers of Traditional China: An Anthology of Poetry
   and Criticism.* Palo Alto, CA: Stanford University
   Press, 2000.

Eger, E. *Bluestockings: Women of Reason from
   Enlightenment to Romanticism.* New York, NY:
   Palgrave MacMillan, 2010.

Flanagan, Sabina. *Hildegard of Bingen: A Visionary
   Life.* New York, NY: Routledge, 1989.

Gilbert, Sandra M., and Susan Gubar. *The Madwoman
   in the Attic: The Woman Writer and the Nineteenth-
   Century Literary Imagination.* New Haven, CT: Yale
   University Press, 1989.

Guessoum, Nidhal. "Muslim Women Scholars in the
   Golden Age" Irtiqa, April 25, 2011. http:/www
   .irtiqa-blog.com/2011/04/muslim-women
   -scholars-in-golden-age.html.

Halton, Charles, and Saana Svärd. *Women's Writing
   of Ancient Mesopotamia: An Anthology of the
   Earliest Female Authors.* New York, NY: Cambridge
   University Press, 2017.

Marotti, Maria. *Italian Women Writers from the
   Renaissance to the Present: Revising the Canon.*
   University Park, PA: The Pennsylvania State
   University Press, 1996.

Martin, Randall. *Women's Writers in Renaissance
   England: An Annotated Anthology.* London and New
   York: Routledge, 2014.

Plant, I. M. *Women Writers of Ancient Greece and Rome: An Anthology.* Norman, OK: University of Oklahoma Press, 2004.

Rothenberg, Jerome. "Enheduanna (2300 BCE.): Seven Sumerian Temple Hymns." *Poems and Poetics*, 2012. https://jacket2.org/commentary/enheduanna-2300-bce-seven-sumerian-temple-hymns.

Wilson, Katharina. *Hrotsvit of Gandersheim: A Florilegium of Her Works.* Rochester, NY: Boydell and Brewer Inc., 1998.

INDEX

About the Author

Anne Cunningham has a PhD in comparative literature. Her areas of scholarship are modernism, women authors and performance artists, and feminist, affect, and queer theory. She has published articles on women modernist writers and feminist theory in academic journals such as *Modern Fiction Studies* and written numerous textbooks on subjects ranging from climate change to women political leaders. She is an Instructor of English at the University of New Mexico in Taos. She is also a published songwriter and lives with her husband and music partner, David Lerner, in Arroyo Hondo, New Mexico.

Photo Credits